Divine Healing
for
Breast Cancer

Bea Dukes
Carlton Dukes, Editor

Dukes Publishing

Divine Healing
for
Breast Cancer

Bea Dukes
Carlton Dukes, Editor

Divine Healing for Breast Cancer

www.DivineHealingforBreastCancer.com

Copyright@2011 by Bea Dukes
Printed in the United States of America.

ISBN 10: 0983354901
ISBN 13: 978-0-9833549-0-1

All rights reserved. No part of this book may be used or reproduced in any manner whatsoever without written permission except in the case of brief quotation embodied in critical articles and reviews. No part of this book may be stored in a database or retrieval system, without prior permission of the author. Making copies of any part of this book for any purpose other than personal use is a violation of U.S. copyright laws.

AUTHOR'S NOTE:
While we have made every effort to provide accurate information in this book, it is possible that omissions and/or errors may have been inadvertently introduced. Because of the dynamic nature of the internet, any web links published in this book, may have changed since publication of this work and may be no longer valid.

COPYRIGHT INFORMATION:
Unless otherwise noted, all Scripture quotations are from the King James Version of the Bible.

Scripture quotations marked "NKJV™" are taken from the New King James Version®. Copyright © 1982 by Thomas Nelson, Inc. Used by permission. All rights reserved.

Scripture taken from the Amplified Bible, Copyright © 1954, 1958, 1962, 1964, 1965, 1987 by The Lockman Foundation. Used by permission.

Scripture quotations marked (NIV) are taken from the Holy Bible, New International Version®, NIV®. Copyright © 1973, 1978, 1984 by Biblica, Inc.™ Used by permission of Zondervan. All rights reserved worldwide. www.zondervan.com

Dedication

This book is dedicated to those who are facing a potential diagnosis of breast cancer, have been diagnosed with breast cancer, or those who may know someone in this situation. It is written to spiritually empower the breast cancer victim and offer Biblical encouragement to everyone touched by this disease.

My hope is that the words written within these pages will be a clarion call to prayer so that God may release a Divine Healing experience within your life and (or) the life of your loved one.

These words are written to empower you and equip you with the tools necessary to seek and to receive Divine Healing!

In all things we give God,
the Glory,
the honor, and
the praise!

*If my people
which are called
by my name
shall humble themselves,
and pray,
and seek my face,
and turn
from their wicked ways;
then will I hear from heaven,
and
will forgive their sin
and
heal their land.*

2 Chronicles 7:14

www.DivineHealingforBreastCancer.com

Contents

Foreword... 11
Acknowledgements.. 13
Introduction..17
Chapter 1 Breast Cancer..21
Chapter 2 Importance of Seven.................................23
Chapter 3 God's Purpose for Your Life.......................33
Chapter 4 Communicating With od............................43
Chapter 5 Increasing Your Faith................................49
Chapter 6 Divine Healing...71
Chapter 7 Healing Meditations for Day 1...................86
Chapter 8 Healing Meditations for Day 2...................96
Chapter 9 Healing Meditations for Day 3.................102
Chapter 10 Healing Meditations for Day 112
Chapter 11 Healing Meditations for Day 5..............121
Chapter 12 Healing Meditations for Day 6..............129
Chapter 13 Healing Meditations for Day 7..............137
Chapter 14 Other Targeted Prayers
    The Lord's Prayer...151
    Prayer before the Biopsy................................152
    Prayer While Waiting for Biopsy Results........154
    Prayer before Surgery....................................156
Bibliography..161
About the Author..164
Additional Information..167

Foreword

There are countless numbers of women that have been healed from breast cancer. I am aware of several who have been blessed with this miracle of Divine Healing.

A pastor, under whose tutelage I served, received God's Divine Healing for breast cancer. What a tremendous blessing after she had received a grave prognosis and after all medical treatments had failed, God delivered her from her distress. Today, she proudly shares her testimony of Divine Healing. She continues to serve proudly in the vocation wherein she has been called to reach the lost. What a tremendous blessing!

Another very dear friend was completely healed of breast cancer and remained cancer free for many years until the Lord called her home to eternal rest. If we were not limited on space, I would go continue to share testimonies of those who have experienced Divine Healing. However, we are very interested in hearing about God's blessing for you.

If you have received Divine Healing for breast cancer, please share your testimonial:
www.DivineHealingforBreastCancer.com.

If you have experienced Divine Healing in another area, please share your experience:
www.HealingTestimonial.com

Acknowledgements

I am very grateful to God for his divine guidance. A special thanks to everyone that helped bring this project together.

I am very appreciative of the support from my dear husband, my soul mate and friend, Carlton, and our wonderful daughter, Mikayla. Thanks for sacrificing those moments of family time to help me deliver this word.

Thanks to all of the spiritual leaders that I have known through the years whose teachings helped shape, mold, and mentor my spiritual growth.

Thanks to all of my extended family. You have always been there for me. Thanks to all of my special friends. You are very special to me and of course "you know who you are."

May God bless all of you!

I remain thankful to God for blessing me with the most wonderful parents in the world, the late Murriell and Geneva Stigall. May their souls rest in peace.

www.DivineHealingforBreastCancer.com

www.HealingTestimonial.com

Even by the God of thy father,
who shall help thee;
and by the Almighty,
who shall bless thee
with blessings of heaven above,
blessings of the deep
that lieth under,
blessings of the breasts,
and of the womb...

Genesis 49:25

Introduction

To everything there is a season, and a time to every purpose under the heaven

Ecclesiastes 3:1

Introduction

Welcome to Divine Healing for Breast Cancer!

It is my sincere hope that God will speak to you through this written word. As Jesus said, "man shall not live by bread alone, but by every "WORD of God" (Luke 4:4)

Over the past several years, God has inspired me to write a series of meditations and prayers based on specific scriptures for particular diseases, conditions, and situations.

Please note that this book is not designed to serve as a substitute for treatment by medical professionals. We are blessed daily with new research that continues to yield scientific discoveries of gigantic proportions as well as advanced technological opportunities far beyond measure.

This book is not a substitute for that, but rather a call on a higher power, God, our heavenly father who is the ultimate source of all being.

Recommend that you read and meditate several times a day.

Perhaps you may wish to meditate and pray in the morning, around noon, and in the afternoon or evening before going to bed.

Introduction

"…….and a time to heal"
Ecclesiastes 3:3

Introduction

You will need to establish regular times for your special communications with God. You can speak to God anytime, but this is your appointed time.

What will be your appointed times?

Let's record them below:

Wk 1: _____   _____   _____

Wk 2: _____   _____   _____

Wk 3: _____   _____   _____

Wk 4: _____   _____   _____

Wk 5: _____   _____   _____

Wk 6: _____   _____   _____

Wk 7: _____   _____   _____

Introduction

You may wish to add weeks in a separate notebook.

If praying like this is new to you, a journal is highly recommended to help keep track of your prayer life. Just as God's graces are renewed every morning, we must also renew our unwavering faith and belief that God will do just what he said! He will meet you at the point of your need!

The Bible tells us that God does not play favorites; he is no respector of persons. Just as people received Divine Healing during the Old Testament and New Testament time periods, we have that same opportunity today. God has that same healing power today. You may wish to read about some of the other Divine Healing experiences:

- Divine Healing of several women from fertility, the first one was Sarah (Gen 17:18-19 and Gen 21:1-7)
- Divine Healing of leprosy - Miriam and Aaron (Numbers 12:1-15)
- Divine Healing of man with withered hand (1 Kings 13:4-6)
- Divine Healing - child raised from death (1 Kings 17:17-24)
- Divine Healing of Naaman's leoprosy (2 Kings 5:1-14)
- Divine Healing of Hezekiah's fatal prognosis (2 Kings 20:1-11)
- The entire book of Job shares the infirmities and tests of Job.
- Many of the Divine Healings from the New Testament are shared throughout this book.

God is the same, yesterday, today and forever more. We need to connect to him and tap into that supernatural reservoir of blessings that He has in store for you! According to your faith, be it unto you!

Chapter 1
Breast Cancer

According to the National Institute of Health, breast cancer affects one in eight women during their lives.

Breast cancer kills more women in the United States than any cancer except lung cancer*.

Worldwide, nearly 1 in 4 women have breast cancer. Over 30% of women are diagnosed after breast cancer has spread beyond the localized stage. Approximately half of them live in highly developed countries

Breast cancer is the kind of cancer that forms in tissues of the breast. It most often forms in the ducts (tubes that carry milk to the nipple) and lobules (glands that make milk).

Breast cancer can occur in both men and women, although male breast cancer is relatively rare.

*No one knows why some women get breast cancer, but there are a number of risk factors.

Chapter 1

Risks that you cannot change include the following:

- Age - the chance of getting breast cancer rises as a woman gets older

- Genes - there are two genes, BRCA1 and BRCA2 that greatly increase the risk.

- Women who have family members with breast or ovarian cancer may wish to be tested.

- Personal factors - beginning periods before age 12 or going through menopause after age 55

*Other risks include being overweight, using hormone replacement therapy, taking birth control pills, drinking alcohol, not having children or having your first child after age 35 or having dense breasts.

Symptoms of breast cancer may include a lump in the breast, a change in size or shape of the breast or discharge from a nipple.

Breast self-exam and mammography can help find breast cancer early when it is most treatable. After you have been diagnosed with breast cancer, your treatments options may vary depending on the kind of breast cancer, the stage of cancer and many other factors.

Note: Regardless of the diagnosis, stage, treatment plan or prognosis, you can seek God for divine healing.

*Data extracted from the U.S. National Institute of Health

Chapter 2
The Importance of 7

Later in this book, we will introduce daily scripture meditations and daily prayers for seven days. This is not an attempt to indicate that it will take seven days for your Divine Healing. It may take seven seconds, seven minutes, or whatever time that God has determined. However, we used the number "7" based on its Biblical significance.

Is the number seven magical? Absolutely not, but prayer changes things! God's willingness to move on your behalf is based on His will for your life. It is not magical whatsoever. There is no earthly power that can be cast toward heaven to compel God's will for you.

The fact that there are "7" daily prayers for breast cancer is based on the importance of the number 7 in the Bible.

✓ The number 7 is very significant as it is used to describe perfection and spiritual completion.

Chapter 2

Chapter 2

- ✓ We can find the number seven at least 735 times in the Bible. Note the 7 in 700 and 7x5 equals 35.
- ✓ Also 7 can be evenly divided into 735 for mathematical purposes without a remainder – nothing left over!
- ✓ The significance of the number seven signals the end of Creation Week in the book of Genesis. (Gen 2:2)

The number continues to bear significance throughout the Bible. For example:

- ❖ Noah took seven clean beasts into the ark by sevens (Genesis 7:2) (He took the unclean beasts 2 by 2.)

- ❖ The seventh time Noah's name is mentioned in the Bible, it is referred to as a perfect man, "Noah was a just man and perfect in his generation" (Genesis 6:9)

- ❖ Seven days pasted after Noah went into the ark before the flood came upon the earth. (Genesis 7:4 and 7:10)

- ❖ The sanctifying blood of the sacrifice was sprinkled seven times (Leviticus 8:11 and Leviticus 14:7)

Chapter 2

- ❖ God ordained every seventh year as a sabbatical year when the land was to lay and rest (Exodus 23:11)

- ❖ The Lord ordained seven days for the sanctification of the altar (Exodus 29:37)

- ❖ As part of the Levitical priesthood, Aaron and his sons were consecrated for seven days before they entered their priestly vocation. (Leviticus 16:14).

- ❖ The Seven Feasts of the Lord exemplify God's use of the complete number of 7:
    - Passover
    - Unleavened Bread
    - First-Fruits
    - Pentecost
    - Atonement
    - Trumpets
    - Tabernacle

- ❖ God ordained every seventh year as a sabbatical year when the land was to lay and rest (Lev 25:2)

Chapter 2

- ❖ When Joshua led the Israelites in battle around the city of Jericho. God gave them specific instructions to march around the city seven times. Then on the seventh day, when they marched, their work was complete as the walls fell and they were victorious on the seventh day (Joshua 6:1-16)
- ❖ It took Solomon seven years to build the temple.
- ❖ Job had seven sons. (Job 42:13)
- ❖ Divine Healing took place when the Prophet Elijah told Naaman to wash seven times in the muddy Jordan River (2 Kings 5:1-19)

- ❖ There were seven appearances of angels during the life of Jesus on earth.

Chapter 2

- To the shepherds (Luke 2:9)
- To Joseph (Matthew 2:13)
- To Joseph (Matthew 2:19)
- After the Temptation (Matthew 4:11)
- In Gethsemane (Luke 22:43.
- At the Resurrection (Matthew 28:2)
- At the Ascension (Acts 1:10)

Chapter 2

❖ **Jesus performed a miracle using only 7 food items** to feed a multitude (two fish and five loaves of bread). His miracle power turned an untenable situation into a manageable one. (Matt 14:17)

❖ **Jesus spoke seven times from the cross.**

1. "Father, forgive them, for they know not what they do" (Luke 23:34) *(Intercessory Prayer to the Father on their behalf)*

2. "Eli, Eli, lama sabachthani?" *meaning my God, my God, why hast thou forsaken me*" (Matthew 27:46)

3. "Verily, I say unto thee today: Thou shalt be with Me in Paradise" (Luke 23:43)

4. "Woman, behold thy son...Behold thy mother" (John 19:26)

5. "I thirst" (John 19:28)

6. "Father, into Thy hand I commend My spirit" (Luke 23:46)

7. "It is finished" (John 19:30)

Chapter 2

- **Seven** good men were chosen to serve in the book of Acts. This included Stephen, a man full of faith and of the Holy Spirit. (Acts 6:1-7)

- The other "beatitudes" blessings of the Lord are found in the Book of Life as the Lord promises special spellings for His people (seven times).

  1. Revelations 1:3
  2. Revelations 14:13
  3. Revelations 16:15
  4. Revelations 19:9
  5. Revelations 20:6
  6. Revelations 22: 7
  7. Revelations 22:14

Read these scriptures at your convenience.

They will bless you indeed.

Chapter 2

- ❖ Revelations, the book of life and the book of completion is also filled with many mentions of **seven** (7):
  - Seven churches
  - Seven spirits
  - Seven golden candlesticks
  - Seven stars
  - Seven lamps
  - Seven seals
  - Seven angels

So you can now see the significance of completeness and spiritual wholeness in terms of seven (7). Therefore, later in this book, we focus on seven days of specific scripture meditations and prayers to consecrate and petition for your healing.

Healing is a form of spiritual, mental, physical, and emotional completeness. Healing of breast cancer is God restoring completeness to your physical body. As we seek God's healing for the breast cancer, we also seek blessings of healing for your entire being: your mind, body, and spirit.

Chapter 2

We will pray for mental fitness, spiritual renewal, and physical healing. God has the power to remove imperfections caused by the cells' DNA mutations. Just as the miracles were performed when Jesus walked on earth, that same power exists today!

Divine healing can make you anew: completely healed, delivered, and set free of the breast cancer. In the world of modern medicine, some forms of cancer have a greater number of treatment options than other forms. But everything on earth is under the authority of God. God can heal you! He can heal every cancerous cell and make you totally cancer free with no toxic cells remaining - nothing left over!

Chapter 3
God's Purpose for Your Life

> "Many are the plans
> in a person's heart,
> but it is the **LORD's purpose**
> that prevails"
>
> Proverbs 19:22 (NIV)

Before we proceed, let's conduct a personal life review to see if you are in your rightful place as God has destined for your life. Write your responses, notes or comments in the spaces below the questions. Now, ask yourself these questions:

Chapter 3

What are your thoughts?

For I know the thoughts that I think toward you, saith the LORD, thoughts of peace, and not of evil, to give you an expected end.
Jeremiah 29:11

Chapter 3

Is my life aligned with God's plan for me?

_____Yes _____No _____Maybe

More importantly, is my life on the path that God has destined for me?

_____Yes _____No _____Maybe

Am I giving and releasing of myself as God desires?

_____Yes _____No _____Maybe

Chapter 3

Do I have any ill feelings toward anyone?

_____Yes   _____No   _____Maybe

Have I forgiven as God has so graciously forgiven me?

_____Yes   _____No   _____Maybe

Is this the life that He has destined for me?

_____Yes   _____No   _____Maybe

Chapter 3

Have I shown positive outreach in the face of humanity's pushback or rejection?

_____Yes _____No _____Maybe

Do I have any illegal or immoral actions resting on my shoulders?

_____Yes _____No _____Maybe

Do I have any unresolved matters that need to be resolved? _____Yes _____No _____Maybe

Chapter 3

Do I have any stressful situations that I simply cannot resolve?

_____Yes   _____No _____Maybe

These are just a few of the questions that you need to ask yourself. Feel free to add others that may be applicable. For example:

- *Do you have any hard feelings about a previous relationship?*

- *What about your family relationships?*

Chapter 3

- *What about your relationships in sports or recreational activities?*

- *What about your relationships with estranged friends?*

- *What about your church relationship?*

Other:

Chapter 3

Please take some time to relax and think about any of your individual circumstances that may present barriers to your particular healing:

_____

_____

_____

_____

_____

_____

_____

If any of the previous questions yield a "maybe" or a "no" response, and fall within your ability to influence, you may want to make every effort to attain peaceful resolution or at least get that situation to a good place.

Ask God to help you determine the ones that are in your will to change and those that are outside of your human ability to influence. Ask God for divine guidance. He will order your steps. Remember to "*cast your cares upon him*" for he cares for you.

Chapter 3

When seeking God's face or when asking for healing, we must have a pure heart and be free of the earthly distractions (weights) that can easily form barriers to our blessings. Do not allow any of the following to block your healing:

- Sin
- Fear
- Pride
- Stress
- Anxiety
- Unbelief
- Frustration
- Lack of Forgiveness

Divine Healing is critical!

Do not allow anything to put your Divine Healing at risk.

Let nothing block your flow!

If we confess our sin, He is faithful and just to forgive us our sins, and to cleanse us from all unrighteousness.
I John 1:9

Chapter 3

Chapter 4
Communicating with God

Before you begin your healing meditations on scriptures and prayers, make sure that you are in a favorable place with God. What is your relationship with God? Only you can answer that.

Your relationship with God is somewhat similar to a relationship with a close friend. If you are not communicating with that friend on a regular basis, a lack of closeness will form. Communication and fellowship is critical to any relationship. We develop a bond with people who share common interests. We form an even closer union with those that we trust and those who are genuinely interested in us. These friends often demonstrate heartfelt care, compassion, and concern about our welfare. It is only with those close knit friends that we may feel comfortable enough to share the sensitive, personal, troubling, and potentially embarrassing areas of our lives.

Chapter 4

Regardless of how long you have known someone, if you do not strengthen the relationship with regular communication, visits, and so forth, it will erode over time. If we do not maintain an active prayer life with God, our spiritual relationship will erode over time.

If you have not spoken with a friend for several months or perhaps years, will you be able to reach that friend? In today's world of technological advances, cell phone numbers change very frequently. So if you are trying to reach someone on a cell phone, the number may have changed since your last conversation.

Our earthly relationships offer some comparison to our relationship with God. If we are not in constant or at least frequent communication with God, distance develops in your spiritual relationship. For that reason, the Bible tells us to "pray without ceasing". We need to maintain a close relationship with God, our Father, and the Creator of all mankind.

On the other hand, our relationship with God is different from our earthly friends in that we know how to find Him at all times. Some people frequently change their email addresses. This most often occurs if the email is connected to a local utility service such as cable or the telephone company.

Click here to contact God

This button simply does not exist. Although we have one of the most mobile societies in the world. So the person that you are trying to reach may no longer reside at the residence that you have on file. The postal service will only forward mail for a specified period of time. Afterwards, mail sent to that addressee may be returned to sender.

It is so refreshing to know that God is not connected to a cell phone. You need not worry about connecting to God (if you think that he is on a different provider line) because God is the ultimate provider! There are no limits on the minutes that you have available for communication with our Savior. There are no roaming charges because He is right there with you. God does not need to appear on the list of your ten most frequently called numbers, because he has a supernatural connection with you and hopefully you are on the same line with your connection back to Him.

It is even more humbling to know that God is not connected to a house number and street address. Letters to God will not be returned to sender. Email messages sent to God will not be returned as undeliverable. God always delivers in "His" divine time. Although we may wait according to "our schedule." He is an on-time God! While the answers to some of our prayers may be delayed, it is all according to God's will. While our address may change, God is always "right there". He is beside us even when we are not aware of his presence. God is with us even in most secret of moments, in closed-door meetings, and in confidential settings. He simply sees and knows everything!

Now, on the other hand, let's go back and look at yet another comparison and contrast of a relationship God and a relationship with an earthly friend. What if your friend offered you one of the most wonderful gifts available? What if at the presentation of that most precious gift you turned

Chapter 4

your back either walked or ran the other way? Then as time passed on, when you realized that you really needed that gift, what if you just boldly walked up and asked for the gift and perhaps for an additional present. How do you think your friend would respond? Well, I can tell you that actions like this, on an earthly basis, will result in hard feelings, anger, rejection, and often retaliatory behavior. However, God is not like mankind. God is so gracious that he forgives us even when we do not deserve it. He sent his only Son to die on the cross and shed his precious blood for the remission of our sins. Jesus paid the ultimate sacrifice on Calvary so that our souls would not be lost. He paid the price and he sits on the right of God the Father, making intercession for us each day. So if you have an active prayer life and have a relationship with God, then you are ready to proceed.

We need only to approach God with a clean heart and surrender ourselves to His will for our lives. Have you surrendered your heart to God? If you have not accepted Christ as your Savior or even if you have, let's pray the prayer of salvation before proceeding.

Chapter 4

*Dear Heavenly Father,
Please forgive me for my sins.
Please create within me a new heart.
I accept you as my Lord and Savior.
I believe that Jesus died on the cross,
was buried, and rose on the third day.
Please save me and help me to live
for you from this day forward.
In Jesus Name, I pray.
Amen*

Chapter 5
Increasing Your Faith

    The benefits of having an intimate relationship with God will enhance your ability to receive your healing. You must believe and trust that the Healing Power of the Holy Spirit can and will heal you of Breast Cancer. God can and will do what He said. God is not a god that He should lie nor shall His word return to him void.

    Write your responses to the questions below:

Do you believe that God **can** and will heal you?

Do you believe that God **wants** to heal you?

Why should **you** receive Divine Healing?

What are some current barriers to your Divine Healing?

Chapter 5

Unforgiveness:

Pride:

Hatred:

Unrighteousness:

Sinful Habits:

Sinful Behavior:

Unbelief:

    If you are seeking a Divine manifestation of the Holy Spirit in your life; or if you are looking for God's Divine Healing power to fully heal you, in addition to other areas

Chapter 5

identified above, you need to search yourself for unbelief and do a faith check. For starters, let's look at your faith level.......

How do you increase your faith level? Well, faith comes by hearing the Word of God. This book is filled with God's word for life and for your current diagnosis. In addition to this book, read your Bible and believe God's word. You may also want to attend a local church if you are physically able. If you cannot, you may wish to listen to Christian music or church via streaming on the internet or on television. You need to let the Word absorb and soak into your mind, body, and spirit.

The most effective way to increase your faith is by reading and studying God's Word. Read and study each of the daily verses and say the prayers. Meditate on the words of the scriptures. Let them soak into your mind and allow your spirit to absorb the words in a special way.

Recommend that you read the meditation verses aloud. Say the scripture meditations and prayers at least three times a time. You can do it more often but do it at least three times a day. The Bible tells us to pray without ceasing.

Chapter 5

We are also advised to avoid vain repetition, but praying God's word is never vain repetition. Giving God's Word back to him in prayer reinforces your relationship and your belief in His Holy Word.

As you read and quote these scriptures back to God, and believe in your heart, stand on the full unwavering power of the Holy Spirit, and do not doubt that God can move on your behalf. Tell God that you will be like Jacob was when he wrestled with the angel, do not let go of God's promised message of healing until He blesses indeed!

Your faith level will often determine the level of your tenacity, perseverance, and the ability to patiently endure until you receive your promised and expected healing. For example, at times, God will heal someone who has very little faith. At times, God will heal someone based on the faith of others as was the Divine Healing of the centurion's servant:

Then Jesus said to the centurion, "Go your way; and as you have believed, so let it be done for you." And his servant was healed that same hour.' Matthew 8:13

Chapter 5

Thus, another instance of Divine Healing! There are times when God recognizes your faith and immediately moves on your behalf as was the case of the crowd:

And when Jesus went out He saw a great multitude; and He was moved with compassion for them, and healed their sick. Matthew 4:14

Another similar example is provided here:

And Jesus departed from thence, and came nigh unto the sea of Galilee; and went up into a mountain, and sat down there. And great multitudes came unto him, having with them those that were lame, blind, dumb, maimed, and many others, and cast them down at Jesus' feet; and he healed them: Insomuch that the multitude wondered, when they saw the dumb to speak, the maimed to be whole, the lame to walk, and the blind to see: and they glorified the God of Israel.

Matthew 15:29-31

Chapter 5

These are clear examples of the expectancy of healing as well as FAITH in action. He wants you to have your faith level built up so that His healing power can flow freely within your mind, body, soul, and spirit.

There were also times when Jesus conducted a check of the person's faith level. Jesus would simply ask the person if they wanted to be healed.

Why do I have to for Divine Healing?

There may be times when you may feel that the treatments for breast cancer have seemingly taken their toll on your natural body, and you may feel like giving up. Just remember that God cares for you. He cares for the fish in the sea and the birds in the air so you know that he surely cares for you.

Sometimes waiting is part of the plan.
Sometimes....
Often times....
Every now and then....
..........waiting is part of the plan.

Chapter 5

Do you recall the lame man who lay by the gate for 38 years?

He simply continued to believe with expectancy.

> **And a certain man was there, which had an infirmity thirty and eight years.**
>
> **⁶When Jesus saw him lie, and knew that he had been now a long time in that case, he saith unto him, Wilt thou be made whole?**
>
> **⁷The (lame) impotent man answered him, Sir, I have no man, when the water is troubled, to put me into the pool: but while I am coming, another steppeth down before me.**
>
> John 5:5-7

Chapter 5

In his case he had an opportunity for Divine Healing only once every year - when an angel would trouble the water.

However, because he was handicapped (lame), he had no one to help him get into his miracle.

Waiting during Year 1:

He had 364 days to wait for that one day for healing of his condition. He waited for the angel to trouble the water at which time, he knew if he could only get into the pool, he would be healed. During those 364 days he needed someone to care for him and to help left his spirits as he

Chapter 5

anxiously waited for his Divine Healing. (Let's pause for a moment to encourage someone who may be waiting for their Divine Healing. Perhaps you have grown tired and feel like giving up. Don't hate your WAIT/WEIGHT. *Remember they that wait upon the Lord shall renew their strength, and if you cast all your care (weights) upon Him, he will carry them for you.*

At the end of year one, the angel came to stir the water (a spirit-moving event), but a person stepped over him into the pool to receive the healing. Now, there he was, so close, there he lay unhealed and frustrated because he had no one to help him into the healing water. So he did not get healed the first year. That being said, he knew that he had yet another three hundred and sixty-four days ahead of him. Can you imagine that?

Waiting during Year 2:

So he waited yet another month, then two, then three…finally six months had passed and then finally it was near the end of his second year. Day after day, week after week, and month after month, his two-year wait nears an

Chapter 5

end. He does not want someone to get in front of him again. What does he need to do to get his healing? What should he do differently to obtain his healing? Is he at the right place? Yes, the angel comes to this particular place, at that particular season, but was he too weak? Did he have the required level of strength needed to get healed? Was his lame condition such that he needed total support?

At the end of year two...... when the angel came yet another person stepped in front of him and received Divine Healing. Another person got healed and he did not. He was simply not in position to get healed? By this time, he had already waited for two years, yet he did not lose hope. He did not lose his faith. Maybe you are asking how does a person get into the right position to be healed?

Waiting during Year 3:

He waited and waited and waited. Minute after minute, hour after hour, perhaps prognosis after prognosis, maybe even day after day, week after week, month after month…..he waited, he waited and yet he waited…..

Chapter 5

During his wait, who was there to give him the love and support that he needed to continue to go through the next 364 days? Will you be there for someone? Will you pray for someone? Will you deliver a gift or a kind word of encouragement? Will you show compassion? This kind of support offers the emotional healing which is required to sustain while waiting. It offers the demonstration of the real power of love. Love is not always about the words you say, but love is also shown by your actions. Will you make a meal or offer transportation? Will you give the caregiver a break so that they can get some rest from the daily 24-hour journey?

At the end of year three...... when the angel came, yet another person stepped in front of him and received their Divine Healing. So we see that another person got healed and he did not. It was just that he did not have the strength to get into the water first. He was simply not in position to get healed. Healing had taken place all around him, but Divine Healing for him had not taken place................................yet!

Chapter 5

You may be in an environment where healing and restoration are taking place all around you. Actually, "you" may appear to be in a neutral state, but do not give up! Perhaps you are saying to yourself, 'how can I get into the right position for my Divine Healing?'

Waiting during Year 4:

He waited yet another year. Minute after minute, hour after hour, perhaps prognosis after prognosis, maybe even day after day, week after week, month after month…..he waited, he waited and yet he waited…..

At the end of the fourth year……. when the angel came, yet another person stepped in front of him and received Divine Healing. Another person got healed and he did not. Yet, he did not give up! He kept his faith because he believed with expectancy that his appointed time for Divine Healing would come "one day."

In his case he had a chance for Divine Healing only once every year - when an angel would trouble the water. But,

Chapter 5

because he was lame, he had no one to help him get into the pool of water for his miracle. If you are reading this book and know someone who needs healing, won't you stand in the gap for that person? Will you be an intercessor? Will you be the one to help propel that individual into her (or his) miracle?

There may be treatment after treatment, week after week, month after month, but don't let go of your faith. Let's take a look at this man's wait for his healing: his wait continued for.......three decades plus eight years. He waited for 38 long years. In today's world, this would have been still.....
.........38 years........... or
.... 456 months....... or
.......1, 976 weeks.......or
.........13,870 days.
What a wait! But when Jesus arrived at the gate, his wait was not in vain! Your wait is not in vain!

Again, as mentioned previously, in his particular case he only had a chance for Divine Healing once a year - when an angel would trouble the water. But, because he was lame, he had no one to help him get into his miracle. If you are reading this book and know someone who needs healing,

Chapter 5

won't you stand in the gap for that person? Will you be an intercessor? Will you be the one to help propel that individual into her or his miracle?

There may be treatment after treatment, week after week, month after month, but don't let go of your faith. Let's take a look at this man's wait for his healing:

In many instances, Jesus proclaimed (confirmed) that it was by a person's very own faith that the healing had taken place. This was the case with the woman who had the blood condition for twelve long years. The Bible tells us that she pressed her way through the multitude of people just to touch the garment of Jesus. Can you imagine being in that condition? I hesitate to think of how she must have felt and often cringe when I think of the way that she was probably treated during that period of history. We obtained this verification from Jesus' words, *"Daughter, be of good comfort; thy faith hath made thee whole. And the woman was made whole from that hour."* (Matthew 9:22)

Instantly she received her Divine Healing because of

her faith. The complete passage follows:

> *And suddenly, a woman who had a flow of blood for twelve years came from behind and touched the hem of His garment.*
> *For she said to herself, "If only I may touch His garment, I shall be made well."*
> *But Jesus turned around, and when He saw her He said,* **"Be of good cheer, daughter; your faith has made you well."** *And the woman was made well from that hour.*
>
> Matthew 9:20-22
"NKJV™"

Remember, the Holy Spirit hath all powers:
- Saving power
- Divine Healing power
- Deliverance power
- Miracle power
- And so much more.
- Allow your faith to take you to the next level!

Chapter 5

This discussion is about a power that is literally beyond human language. If you can get your faith to operate at a higher level, then God can manifest greater miracles either to you or through you or on someone else's behalf. Healing does take place through intercession. This is similar to being healed based on the faith of another individual. I am not comfortable with the idea of relying on someone else's faith for a critical healing. How about you?

> *And this is the confidence that we have in …..Him that, if we ask any thing according to …..His will He heareth us: ……And if we know that he hears us, ….. Whatsoever we ask, ……we know that we have the petitions that --…… we desired of him.*
> I John 5:14-15

Let's take a moment and record the status of your Faith. Your faith shall be renewed …just as his graces are renewed every morning….

Chapter 5

Day 1:

Day 2:

Day 3:

Chapter 5

Day 4:

Day 5:

Day 6:

Day 7:

(You may wish to use an additional journal or notebook if necessary.)

Chapter 5

The Prayer of Faith

Is anyone among you in trouble?
…..Let them pray.
…..Is anyone happy?
…..Let them sing songs of praise.
…..Is anyone among you sick?

Let them call the elders of the church to pray over them and anoint them with oil in the name of the Lord.

And the prayer offered in faith will make the sick person well; the Lord will raise them up.
…..If they have sinned,
…..they will be forgiven.

Therefore confess your sins to each other and pray for each other so that you may be healed.
The prayer of a righteous person is powerful and effective.

James 5:13-16
(NIV)

Chapter 5

We cannot close the discussion of this chapter without.........

.....a committment to your Declaration of Faith

......and a commitment to pray the prayer of faith on a regular basis.

The prayer of faith is important as is the prayer of supplication and the spiritual warfare prayer that will follow for each day...

Chapter 5

DECLARATION OF FAITH

I, _____(name)

on _____(date)

do hereby declare that I am in complete agreement with God's Word that these Scriptures are in full operation in my life. God's Word is life to me and health to all my flesh!

I declare it is done in Jesus' Name.

It is finished!

Amen.

Chapter 6

*Release yourself
into the arms of Jesus
for He cares for you!*

Chapter 6

Divine Healing

Divine Healing is healing that takes place under the divine power of the Holy Spirit. Note, Divine Healing is not always synonymous with healing our way. It is healing God's way!

Often healing does not take place as we expect for various reasons. When Jesus performed only a few miracles because of the people's unbelief, he left the town and wiped the dust from his feet (Mark 6). It was not that He had lost power because He was God in the flesh. That being said, He had all power, but the miracles could not be performed simply due to their unbelief. It was then that Jesus simply wiped his feet and moved on to a place where faith was active and unwavering. In that town, there was a spiritual power outage caused by lack of faith (their unbelief).

Chapter 6

We manage and control so many things in life, but we can never tell God how to be God. God is omnipotent, omniscient, and omnipresent. Because He is a sovereign God, he relies on no other power or beings. The conditions must be right for healing to take place. This was the case when Jesus went to Bethsaida and had to relocate the man for the manifestation of his healing. We will further discuss this situation later in this chapter.

Divine Healing can also take place in many different venues or ways including Divine Healing through Faith as we discussed in Chapter 6. Divine Healing can also manifest through the laying on of hands as Jesus often demonstrated. Divine Healing also occurs through spiritual deliverance, through the breaking of curses, through prayer and fasting, through the gift of healing, through the power of transference (healing cloths), and simply through God's holy presence.

Let's look briefly at a demonstration of Divine Healing through the laying on of hands. Jesus gave Divine Healing power to his disciples. This power had the ability to cast out unclean spirits, and heal all kinds of sicknesses and diseases (Matthew 10:1).

Chapter 6

Before He died, was buried, and rose from the grave, Jesus spoke prophetically about the power that would also come later for all who believed.

And these signs shall follow them that believe; In my name shall they cast out devils; they shall speak with new tongues;

……..**they shall lay hands on the sick, and they shall recover.** Mark 16:17-18

We are also instructed about the laying on of hands in James 5:14-16 as shown below:

Is anyone among you sick?
Let him call for the elders of the church, and let them pray over him, anointing him with oil in the name of the Lord.
And the **prayer of faith** *will save the sick, and the Lord will raise him up.*
And if he has committed sins, he will be forgiven. Confess your trespasses to one another, and pray for one another, that you may be healed.
The effective, fervent prayer of a righteous man avails much.

Chapter 6

Let's look briefly at a demonstration of Divine Healing through spiritual deliverance. There are times when an illness is caused by a demonic spirit. In this case, the person must be delivered of the demonic presence or generational curse and Divine Healing comes forth speedily.

However, the level of FAITH (Chapter 6) and the casting out of demons are in direct correlation with each other. For example:

> *...And, behold, a woman of Canaan came out of the same coasts, and cried unto him, saying,* **Have mercy on me, O Lord, thou son of David; my daughter is grievously vexed with a devil.**
> *...But he answered her not a word. And his disciples came and besought him, saying, Send her away; for she crieth after us.*
> *...But he answered and said, I am not sent but unto the lost sheep of the house of Israel.*
> *...Then came she and worshipped him, saying, Lord, help me.*

Chapter 6

... Then Jesus answered and said unto her, **O woman, great is thy faith: be it unto thee even as thou wilt. And her daughter was made whole from that very hour.**
Excerpts from Matthew 15:22-28

Here we witnessed another demonstration of Divine Healing that occurred instantaneously. This woman's daughter was possessed with a demonic spirit and Jesus healed her because of the Mother's faith. The healing did not occur because of the daughter's faith, but it was because her Mother cared enough to seek the very best for her daughter – Divine Healing from Jesus that resulted in her being healed that very moment.

Many people are ill because of demonic spirits that have taken up residence in their bodies. This was Mary Magdalene's problem. She was possessed with evil spirits and illness, but Jesus healed her. *"And certain women, which had been healed of evil spirits and infirmities, Mary called Magdalene, out of whom went* **seven** *devils"* (Luke 8:2)

Chapter 6

The same day that Jesus healed the fever that plagued Peter's mother-in-law, they brought many people to Him who were possessed with devils, "He cast out the spirits with his WORD, and healed all that were sick." (Matthew 8:16) In this case, Jesus commanded the demons to leave using his WORD. You have that same power to command the demonic spirits to leave and return no more.

There are times when we experience generational curses. Today's physicians will always ask about your family's medical history. If your parents had certain conditions, scientifically speaking, you may have a higher propensity of developing certain conditions based on your genetic composition, diet, and other risk factors. Jesus also delivered us from the curse of the law. We are blessed and not cursed. We are healed from the curses in Jesus Name (Galatians 3:13).

You will be able to exercise this kind of command language in your daily prayers that appears in the latter chapters of this book.

Let's look briefly at a demonstration of Divine Healing through prayer and fasting. When Jesus walked here on earth, with the disciples, he was in such demand that

Chapter 6

his disciples often conducted Divine Healings among the people. However, there was at least one particular situation, where the demonic presence did not respond directly to their power. In fact, Jesus informed the disciples that "this power" came only by fasting and prayer.

You may recall that Jesus prayed often. He even went on a sabbatical and prayed in the wilderness forty days and forty nights. There were times when his disciples perhaps grew weary of his rigorous prayer life. I recall the example when the disciples fell fast asleep after Jesus had given them explicit instructions, *"Watch ye here, while I pray"* (Matthew 26:36) The bottom line is this: in some cases, Divine Healing may only come by fasting and prayer:

> *...And when they were come to the multitude, there came to him a certain man, kneeling down to him, and saying,*
> *...Lord, have mercy on my son: for he is lunatick, and sore vexed: for ofttimes he falleth into the fire, and oft into the water.*
> **...And I brought him to thy disciples and they could not cure him.**

Chapter 6

…Then Jesus answered and said, O faithless and perverse generation, how long shall I be with you? how long shall I suffer you? bring him hither to me.

…And **Jesus rebuked the devil; *and* he departed out of him: and the child was cured from that very hour.**

…Then came the disciples to Jesus apart, and said, why could not we cast him out?

…And Jesus said unto them, Because of your unbelief: for verily I say unto you, If ye have faith as a grain of mustard seed, ye shall say unto this mountain, Remove hence to yonder place; and it shall remove; and nothing shall be impossible unto you.

*…***Howbeit this kind goeth not out but by prayer and fasting.*** (Matthew 17:13-21)

Let's look briefly at a demonstration of Divine Healing through the gift of healing…

…There are different kinds of gifts, but the same Spirit distributes them.

…There are different kinds of service, but the same Lord.

Chapter 6

...There are different kinds of working, but in all of them and in everyone it is the same God at work.
...Now to each one the manifestation of the Spirit is given for the common good. ......To one there is given through the Spirit a message of wisdom,
......to another a message of knowledge by means of the same Spirit,
...to another faith by the same Spirit,
...to another gifts of healing by that one Spirit,
...to another miraculous powers, to another prophecy,
...to another distinguishing between spirits, to another speaking in different kinds of tongues
... and to still another the interpretation of tongues
...All these are the work of one and the same Spirit, and he distributes them to each one, just as he determines.
I Corinthians 12: 4-11

Let's review a demonstration of Divine Healing through transference. There are many people who are skeptical about prayer cloths, handkerchiefs, and so forth. Jesus' garments were so filled with the Holy Spirit that many were healed simply by the touching of his garment (cloth).. As discussed in Chapter 6, although the woman with the issue of blood touched the garment of Jesus, she received Divine Healing because of her faith. We obtained this verification from Jesus' words, "*Daughter, be of good comfort; thy faith hath made thee whole. And the woman was made whole from that hour.*" (Matthew 9:22) Instantly she received her Divine Healing because of her faith.

Yet many were healed and are still being healed by Divine Healing transference.

…..And when the men of that place had knowledge of him, they sent out into all that country round about, and brought unto him all that were diseased;

….And besought him that they might only touch the hem of his garment: **and as many as touched were made perfectly whole.**

Matthew 14:35-36

After the Apostle Paul's' conversion, God used him mightily. He was also blessed in the gift of healing as shown in this passage:

And God wrought special miracles by the hands of Paul:

So that from his body were brought unto the sick handkerchiefs or aprons, and the

Chapter 6

diseases departed from them, and the evil spirits went out of them. Acts 19:11-12

Divine Healing can take place in many forms. Although it may occur suddenly or instantaneously, sometimes Divine Healing may come in phases or through a series of steps, phases, or methods depending on the particular situation.

Divine Healing Requires Flexibility
How to be flexible in a non-flexible situation?

When you have just received a diagnosis of Stage 1, Stage 2, Stage 3, or Stage 4, your world has most likely just flipped upside down. What will I do? How can this be? Why me? The emotions run rampant. The thoughts are endless and the decisions are upon you. You do not need to go through this alone. We have a Savior who cares for you. He will never leave you nor forsake you. Cast your cares upon Him because He really does care for you. To be healed you need an open mind, strong faith, and you must remain flexible in a seemingly non-flexible situation.

Chapter 6

God may heal you immediately!

God can and that is just what He may do. Sometimes we have to become flexible and relocate from where we are to another place for the complete healing. We must always be led by the Spirit so that relocation may be in the form of a mental relocation (changing how you see the world), i.e. changing your mental picture. That relocation may be a spiritual one, as we grow spiritually, we move from faith to faith and from glory to glory. That relocation may be a physical one.

Sometimes our environment makes us sick. God will not take you to a place where His grace is not sufficient for you. God may open a door for you to relocate to receive a different treatment or he may create an opportunity for you to travel to a different treatment center. Be open to the will and leading of God. The Great Physician may need you to relocate from one physician to another for a second opinion. There He may open your eyes to a new or improved diagnosis. Whatever the situation, at a time like this, we need to yield to the call of God.

What if God does not heal me immediately?

So if God does not heal immediately, it may be for several reasons, one of which is unresolved sin that interrupts the flow of the Holy Spirit and it could be due to unbelief. Maybe your faith level is not up to the level that God requires, maybe you are surrounded by unbelievers or those of little faith or maybe you are expecting God to move in one way and He is ready to move in a different way and maybe it is just timing. Remember to remain open and listen to the voice of God.

Wherever Jesus and his disciples traveled, a crowd was always nearby waiting to hear his teachings and to be healed. Get in the crowd, get in the press, and be willing to press into what God has just for you. Again, this was the very case on the day that he went to Bethsaida, the crowd brought a blind man to Jesus. They had heard of His healing power, so they just wanted Jesus to touch the blind man and asked Jesus to do just that. But guess what, Jesus did not do as they had specifically requested and expected, but rather, *"He took the blind man by the hand and led him outside the village. When he had spit on the man's eyes and put his hands on him, Jesus asked, "Do you see anything?" He looked up and said, "I see people; they look like trees walking around." Once more Jesus put his hands on the man's eyes. Then his eyes were opened, his sight was restored, and he saw everything clearly."* (Mark 8:22-25)   In this scenario, Jesus moved the man outside of where he was, he did something different and actually spat on the man's eyes. This must have been an eye-opening experience! Jesus not only spat on his eyes leaving transference of himself, but He also laid hands on the man.

What if your Divine Healing takes place in phases?
The man's healing was not immediate but rather in phases as he gradually regained his sight and saw rather blurry as explained by "men looking like trees". Then, when Jesus laid his hands on him a second time, **the man's eyes were clearly opened and his sight was restored.** What a blessing of Divine Healing!

Chapter 6

Let's talk about your responses to these questions:

What if the man had not spoken truthfully about his partial healing (*i.e. seeing people as tall trees*)?

What if he had been angry because Jesus spat on him?

What if the man had been prideful and demanded that Jesus merely touch him as the crowd insisted? (*i.e. wanting Divine Healing his way*)

What if God is healing you through the medications?

What if the Spirit of God is leading you to seek other options?

What if God decides to heal you through the prescribed treatment plan? (Or perhaps even something new?)

What if your Divine Healing manifests over time?

Will you continue to seek your Divine Healing?

Will you hold onto your faith?

Have Faith in God!

The Daily Prayers for Divine Healing

These prayers include the prayer of petition and prayer of spiritual warfare.

Chapter 7 - Day 1

Get ready for your miracle……

Day 1

Meditations and Prayers
God's Word for Worship

Every day, worship the Lord! Exalt Him above everything!

Worship the LORD your God and
His blessing will be on your food and water.
I will take away sickness from among you

Exodus 23:25

God's Word for your Fear

It's only natural that we have human fears, but ......

Be strong and courageous.
Do not be afraid or terrified because of them,
For the LORD your God goes with you;
He will never leave you nor forsake you."

Deuteronomy 31:6
(NIV)

Chapter 7 - Day 1

God's Word for Obedience

If thy wilt diligently hearken to the voice of the Lord thy God, and wilt do that which is right in his sight, an wilt give ear to his commandments, and keep all his statutes, I will put none of these diseases upon thee, which I have brought upon the Egyptians: for I am the Lord that healeth thee.

Exodus 15:26

Chapter 7 - Day 1

God's Word for your Faith

*The key to receiving your healing is that your faith level
Must be present, active, and unwavering.*

Now faith is the substance of things hoped for,
the evidence of things not seen.

Hebrews 11:1

*Verily I say unto you,
If ye have faith as a grain of mustard seed,
Ye shall say unto this mountain,
Remove hence to yonder place;
And it shall remove; and
Nothing shall be impossible unto you.*
Matthew 17:20

*Meditate on this word....
...let it soak into your spirit*

Chapter 7 - Day 1

God's Covenant Word for your Healing

¹If you will listen diligently to the voice of the Lord your God, being watchful to do all His commandments which I command you this day,

The Lord your God will set you high above all the nations of the earth.

²And all these blessings shall come upon you and overtake you if you heed the voice of the Lord your God.

³Blessed shall you be in the city and blessed shall you be in the field.

⁴Blessed shall be the fruit of your body and the fruit of your ground and the fruit of your beasts, the increase of your cattle and the young of your flock.

⁵Blessed shall be your basket and your kneading trough.

⁶Blessed shall you be when you come in and blessed shall you be when you go out.

⁷The Lord shall cause your enemies who rise up against you to be defeated before your face; they shall come out against you one way and flee before you seven ways.

Chapter 7 - Day 1

⁸The Lord shall command the blessing upon you in your storehouse and in all that you undertake. And He will bless you in the land which the Lord your God gives you.

⁹The Lord will establish you as a people holy to Himself, as He has sworn to you, if you keep the commandments of the Lord your God and walk in His ways.

¹⁰And all people of the earth shall see that you are called by the name [and in the presence of] the Lord, and they shall be afraid of you.

¹¹And the Lord shall make you have a surplus of prosperity, through the fruit of your body, of your livestock, and of your ground, in the land which the Lord swore to your fathers to give you.

¹²The Lord shall open to you His good treasury, the heavens, to give the rain of your land in its season and to bless all the work of your hands; and you shall lend to many nations, but you shall not borrow.

¹³And the Lord shall make you the head, and not the tail; and you shall be above only, and you shall not be beneath, if you heed the commandments of the

Chapter 7 - Day 1

Lord your God which I command you this day and are watchful to do them.

¹⁴And you shall not turn aside from any of the words which I command you this day, to the right hand or to the left, to go after other gods to serve them
Deuteronomy 28:1-14
Amplified Bible

And when He had called His twelve disciples
To Him, He gave them power
Over unclean spirits,
……..to cast them out,
……..and to **heal** *all manner (kinds) of sickness*
…….and all manner (kinds) of disease.
Matthew 10:1

God is not a man.
God does not lie.
Let's go to war against your situation!

Chapter 7 - Day 1

Prayer

Dear Heavenly Father,

I praise thee oh God! I exalt you above the heavens and the earth! I confess any sin in my heart today. I pray that you will forgive my sins and restore me anew. Thank you for every blessing.

Father, I have been diagnosed with Stage __ Breast Cancer. Medically speaking, this is a difficult condition. I am aware that nothing is impossible for you. My body is the temple of the Holy Spirit.

In the name of Jesus, I rebuke every cancer cell that may have formed from a hereditary spirit. I command it to leave my body right now.

In the name of Jesus, I bind every foul spirit that may have formed from stress, from pride or from conditions unknown to me. I cast it into the pit from whence it shall never return. I loose complete healing. Breast Cancer you must go! I command you to go in Jesus Name!

Thank you for healing me! Thank you for restoring me.

In Jesus Name I pray, Amen.

Day 2

Please all your cares on Him.....

Chapter 8 - Day 2

God's Word for Worship

Every day, worship the Lord! Exalt Him above everything!

Worship the LORD your God, and his
blessing will be on your food and water.
I will take away sickness from among you,

Exodus 23:25

God's Word for your Fear

It's only natural that we have human fears, but ……

So do not fear, for I am with you;
do not be dismayed, for I am your God.
I will strengthen you and help you;
I will uphold you
with my righteous right hand.
Isaiah 41:10

Day 2

God's Word for Obedience

Ye shall diligently keep the commandments of the LORD your God, and his testimonies, and his statutes, which he hath commanded thee.

And thou shalt do that which is right and good in the sight of the LORD: that it may be well with thee, and that thou mayest go in and possess the good land which the LORD sware unto thy fathers.

To cast out all thine enemies from before thee, as the LORD hath spoken.

Deuteronomy 6:17-19

And this is love:
That we walk in obedience to his commands.
As you have heard from the beginning,
His command is that you walk in love.

2 John 6 (NIV)

Chapter 8 - Day 2

God's Word for your Faith

The key to receiving your healing is that your faith level must be present, active, and unwavering.

And, behold, a woman, which was diseased with an issue of blood twelve years, came behind him, and touched the hem of his garment:

For she said within herself, If I may but touch his garment, I shall be whole.

But Jesus turned him about, and when he saw her, he said, Daughter, be of good comfort; thy faith hath made thee whole. And the woman was made whole from that hour.

Matthew 9:20-22

Chapter 8 - Day 2

God's Word for your Healing

Surely he hath borne our griefs, and carried our sorrows: yet we did esteem him stricken, smitten of God, and afflicted.

But he was wounded for our transgressions,
he was bruised for our iniquities: the chastisement
of our peace was upon him; and with his stripes we are **healed**.

Isaiah 53:4-5
(NIV)

*And Jesus went about all Galilee,
teaching in their synagogues,
preaching the gospel of the kingdom,
and* **healing** *all kinds of sickness
and all kinds of disease among the people.*

Matthew 4:23
"NKJV™"

Chapter 8 - Day 2

Prayer

Dear Heavenly Father,
Thou art my refuge and strength, you are a very present help in trouble! Thou art the God above all! I praise thee oh God! I exalt you above the heavens and the earth! I confess any sin in my heart today. I pray that you will forgive my sins and restore me anew. Thank you for every blessing.

My body is the temple of the Holy Spirit. In the name of Jesus, I break every curse of breast cancer, sickness and disease from my body. Breast Cancer you must go, in Jesus Name!

I believe God's Word for the miracle of Divine Healing in my life!

I release the miracle of Divine Healing in my life today.
By His stripes, I am healed.
In the name of the Father, Son and Holy Spirit…
Amen

DAY 3

With expectation, prepare to receive your miracle!

Day 3
God's Word for Worship

Every day, worship the Lord!
Exalt Him above everything!

With long life I will satisfy him,
and show him my salvation.

Psalms 91:16
"NKJV™"

Chapter 9 - Day 3

God's Word for your Fear
It's only natural that we have human fears, but ……

And David said to Solomon his son,

Be strong and of good courage, and do it:

Fear not, nor be dismayed:

…….for the LORD God,

…….even my God,

…….will be with thee;

……..he will not fail thee,

………nor forsake thee,

………until thou hast finished all the work for

……..the service of the house of the LORD

I Corinthians 28:20

Chapter 9 - Day 3

God's Word for Obedience

"If you love Me, Keep My commandments."

John 14:15

Chapter 9 - Day 3

God's Word for your Faith

The key to receiving your healing is that your faith level must be present, active, and unwavering.

Therefore, the promise comes by faith, so that it may be by grace and may be guaranteed to all Abraham's offspring - not only to those who are of the law but also to those who are of the faith of Abraham. He is the father of us all.

As it is written: I have made you a father of many nations. He is our father in the sight of God, in whom he believed - the God who gives life to the dead and calls things that are not as though they were.

Against all hope, Abraham in hope believed and so became the father of many nations, just as it had been said to him, "So shall your offspring be."

Without weakening in his faith, he faced the fact that his body was as good as dead - since he was about a hundred years old - and that Sarah's womb was also dead. Yet he

Chapter 9 - Day 3

did not waver through unbelief regarding the promise of God, but was strengthened in his faith and gave glory to God, being fully persuaded that God had power to do what he had promised.
Romans 4:16-21

Chapter 9 - Day 3

God's Word for your Healing

*...for it is God who works in you to will
and to act according to his good purpose.*

Philippians 2:13

Do not be anxious about anything, but in everything, by prayer and petition, with thanksgiving, present your requests to God. And the peace of God, which transcends all understanding, will guard your hearts and your minds in Christ Jesus.

Philippians 4:6-7

**For God hath not given us
the spirit of fear;
but of power, and of love,
and of a sound mind.**

II Timothy 1:7

Chapter 9 - Day 3

Chapter 9 - Day 3

Let us hold unswervingly to the hope we profess,
For he who promised is faithful.
Hebrews 10:23

**So do not throw away your confidence;
It will be richly rewarded.**
Hebrews 10:35 (NIV)

Jesus Christ is the same
Yesterday and today and forever.
Hebrews 13:8

Who his own self bare our sins in his own body on the tree that we, being dead to sins, should live unto righteousness: by whose stripes ye were healed.
I Peter 2:24

Chapter 9 - Day 3

Prayer

Dear Heavenly Father,

I praise thee oh God! How great is our God! I exalt you above the heavens and the earth! I confess any sin in my heart today.

I pray that you will forgive my sins and restore me anew. Thank you for everything blessing. My body is the temple of the Holy Spirit.

In the name of Jesus, I rebuke every cancerous cell that may have entered my body through witchcraft, disobedience, or by some cause unknown to me.
I come against breast cancer in the Name of Jesus. Breast Cancer you must go, in Jesus Name! I believe God's Word for the miracle of Divine Healing in my life!

By His stripes, I am completely healed.
Thank you for healing me.
In Jesus Name I pray,
Amen

Day 4

Trust God for your divine healing!

Day 4

Stand firmly on the Word of God!

Day 4
God's Word for Worship

Every day, worship the Lord! Exalt Him above everything!

O come, let us sing unto the Lord:
Let us make a joyful noise to the rock of our salvation. Let us come before his presence with thanksgiving, and make a joyful noise unto him with psalms.
For the Lord is a great God,
And a great King above all gods
Psalms 95:1-3

God's Word for your Fear

It's only natural that we have human fears, but ......

For God hath not given us the spirit of fear;
But of power,
And of love,
And of a sound mind.

2 Timothy 1:7

Chapter 10 - Day 4

God's Word for Obedience

Therefore everyone who hears these words of mine
.........and puts them into practice
.... is like a wise man
.........who built his house on the rock.
.........The rain came down,
.........the streams rose,
.........and the winds blew
.........and beat against that house;
.........yet it did not fall,
.........because it had its foundation on the rock

Matthew 7:24-25

Chapter 10 - Day 4

God's Word for Obedience

Therefore everyone who hears these words of mine
.........and puts them into practice
.... is like a wise man
.........who built his house on the rock.
.........The rain came down,
.........the streams rose,
.........and the winds blew
.........and beat against that house;
.........yet it did not fall,
.........because it had its foundation on the rock

Matthew 7:24-25

Chapter 10 - Day 4

God's Word for your Faith

*The key to receiving your healing
is that your faith level
must be present, active, and unwavering.*

**So then FAITH comes by hearing,
……..and hearing by the word of God.**
Romans 10:17

*Doers of the Word are blessed….
Not hearers of the Word
So activate your Faith by doing what
God (His Word) is telling you to do!*

Chapter 10 - Day 4

God's Word for your Healing

The LORD will keep you
.... free from every disease.
.........He will not inflict on you
........the horrible diseases you knew in Egypt...

Deuteronomy 7:15

O LORD my God,
I cried unto thee, and thou hast healed me

Psalms 30:2

Have mercy on me, O LORD

Psalms 6:2
"NKJV™"

Chapter 10 - Day 4

Chapter 10 - Day 4

Prayer

Dear Heavenly Father,

I praise thee oh God! I exalt you above the heavens and the earth!

Thank you for every blessing. I confess any sin in my heart today.

I pray that you will forgive my sins and restore me anew.

My body is the temple of the Holy Spirit. My body is the temple of the Holy Spirit.

In the name of Jesus, I break every generational curse from my body, from my household, and from my family. I speak to breast cancer and every hidden disease, be thou removed and cast into the sea.

Breast Cancer you must go, in Jesus Name! I believe God's Word for the miracle of Divine Healing in my life! By His stripes, I am healed.

In the name of the Father, Son, and Holy Spirit,
Amen.

Day 5

Trust God for your divine healing!

Day 5
God's Word for Worship

Every day, worship the Lord!
Exalt Him above everything!

But the hour cometh, (and now is that time)!
...... when the true worshippers
...... shall worship the Father in spirit and in truth:
...... for the Father seeketh such to worship him.
...... God is a Spirit:
......and they that worship him
......must worship him in spirit and in truth
John 4:23-24

Chapter 11 - Day 5

God's Word for your Fear

It's only natural that we have human fears, but ……

Fear not, O land;

……… be glad and rejoice:

……… for the LORD will do great things

Joel 2:21

Chapter 11 - Day 5

God's Covenant Word for Obedience

*This day I call heaven and earth
.. as witnesses against you
...that I have set before you
...life and death,
...blessings and curses.*

*Now choose life, so that you and your children
......may live and that you may love
......the LORD your God,
.....listen to his voice,
.....and hold fast to him.
.....For the LORD is your life,
.....and he will give you many years in the land
.... he swore to give to your fathers,
.... Abraham, Isaac and Jacob.*

Deuteronomy 30:19-20

Chapter 11 - Day 5

God's Word for your Faith
The key to receiving your healing is that your faith level must be increased

Let Him have all your worries and cares,
.....for He is always thinking about you
.....and watching everything that concerns you.

1 Peter 5:7
NLT

The Word of God will strengthen your FAITH……

Chapter 11 - Day 5

God's Word for your Healing

For I will restore health unto thee,
...... and I will heal thee of thy wounds,
......saith the LORD
Jeremiah 30:17

I shall not die, but live, and declare the works of the LORD.
Psalms 118:17

That it might be fulfilled which was spoken

By Esaias the prophet, saying,

Himself took our infirmities,

And bare our sicknesses.
Matthew 8:17

Chapter 11 - Day 5

Chapter 11 - Day 5

Prayer

Dear Heavenly Father,

I praise thee oh God! I exalt you above the heavens and the earth! I confess any sin in my heart today.

I pray that you will forgive my sins and restore me anew. Thank you for every blessing. My body is the temple of the Holy Spirit. In the name of Jesus,

I break every curse of sickness, disease, infirmity, breast cancer, and premature death from my body and cast it into the sea that it shall come no more.

Breast Cancer you must go, in Jesus Name! I believe God's Word for the miracle of Divine Healing in my life. By His stripes, I am healed. Just as your graces are renewed every morning, so shall my healing break forth!

In the name of the Father, Son and Holy Spirit,
Amen

Day 6

While God is working this out for you....

Speak those things that be not as though they are......

Speak "Healing" over your life!

Day 6

God's Word for Worship

Every day, worship the Lord!
Exalt Him above everything!

Praise the LORD, O my soul,
And forget not all his benefits—
Who forgives all your sins
And heals all your diseases

Psalms 103:3

Chapter 12 - Day 6

God's Word for your Fear
It's only natural that we have human fears, but ......

But when Jesus heard it, he answered him, saying,
..........."Fear not: believe only,
..........and she shall be made whole.
                    Luke 8:50

God's Word for Obedience

If you obey my commands, you will remain in my love,
.......just as I have obeyed my Father's commands
.......and remain in his love.
.......I have told you this so that my joy may be in you
.......and that your joy may be complete.
.... My command is this
.......Love each other as I have loved you.
                    John 15:10-12

Chapter 12 - Day 6

God's Word for your Faith

**The key to receiving your healing
is that your faith level
must be present, active, and unwavering.**

Looking unto Jesus

…..the author and finisher of our faith;

…..who for the joy that was set before him

…..endured the cross,

…..despising the shame, and is set down

…..at the right hand of the throne of God.
Hebrews 12:2

Chapter 12 - Day 6

"I am the way, the truth and the LIFE"
John 14:6

Chapter 12 - Day 6

God's Word for your Healing

I shall not die, but live, and declare the works of the LORD.
Psalms 118:17

And the whole multitude
Sought to touch Him,
For power went out from Him
And healed them all
Luke 6:19
"NKJV™"

Chapter 12 - Day 6

Prayer

Dear Heavenly Father,

O Lord, God Almighty, there is none like you!

Your love and faithfulness surrounds me.

I praise thee oh God! I exalt you above the heavens and the earth! I confess any sin in my heart today.

I pray that you will forgive my sins and restore me anew.

Thank you for every blessing.

My body is the temple of the Holy Spirit.

In the name of Jesus, I speak to cancer and to any other cell in my body that maybe infected.

Be though removed and cast into the sea.

Cancer you must go, in Jesus Name!

Chapter 12 - Day 6

I believe God's Word for the miracle of Divine Healing in my life.

By His stripes, I am healed.

Just as your graces are renewed every morning, so shall my FAITH remain strong and so shall my DIVINE HEALING break forth!

In the name of the Father, Son, Holy Spirit, and Jesus Christ our Lord,

Amen

Chapter 13 - Day 7

Day 7
Believe.....

Day 7

God's Word for Worship

Every day, *worship the Lord!* ***Exalt Him above everything****! Even in your sickness, regardless of how you feel… even on your worst days exalt the Lord and say………..*

**I will bless the Lord
at all times:
His praise
shall continually
be in my mouth**

Psalms 34:1

Chapter 13 - Day 7

God's Word for your Fear
It's only natural that we have human fears, but ......

Indeed, the very hairs of your head are all numbered.
Don't be afraid;
You are worth more than many sparrows
Luke 12:17

Chapter 13 - Day 7

God's Word for Obedience

**Obedience
is better than sacrifice,
And submission
is better than
Offering the fat of rams**

I Samuel 15:22

Chapter 13 - Day 7

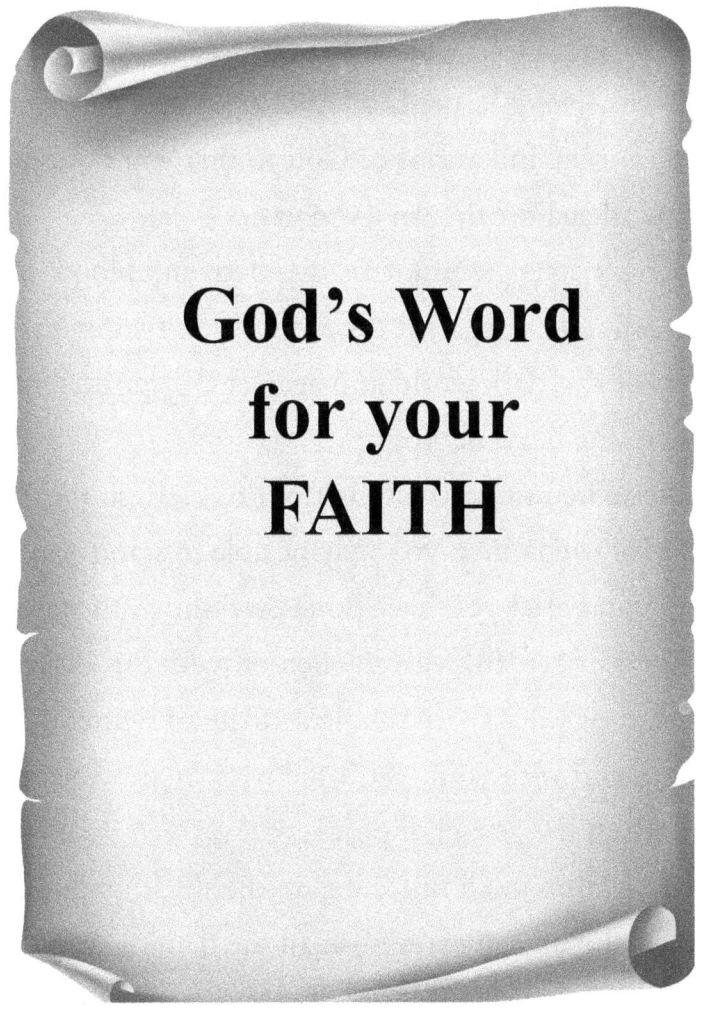

God's Word for your FAITH

Chapter 13 - Day 7

God's Word for your Faith

The key to receiving your healing is that your faith level must be present, active, and unwavering.

Finally, be strong in the Lord and in his mighty power.
…..Put on the full armor of God so that you can take your stand against the devil's schemes.
…..For our struggle is not against flesh and blood, but against the rulers, against the authorities, against the powers of this dark world and against the spiritual forces of evil in the heavenly realms.
…..Therefore put on the full armor of God, so that when the day of evil comes, you may be able to stand your ground, and after you have done everything, to stand.
…..Stand firm then, with the belt of truth buckled around your waist, with the breastplate of righteousness in place, and with your feet fitted with the readiness that comes from the gospel of peace.
…..In addition to all this, take up the shield of faith, with which you can extinguish all the flaming arrows of the evil one. Take the helmet of salvation and the sword of the Spirit, which is the word of God.

Ephesians 6:10-17(NIV)

Chapter 13 - Day 7

Chapter 13 - Day 7

God's Word for your Healing

For I will restore health unto thee, and I will heal thee of thy wounds, saith the LORD;

Jeremiah 30:17

When thou passest through the waters,
I will be with thee;
And through the rivers,
They shall not overflow thee:
When thou walkest through the fire,
Thou shalt not be burned;
Neither shall the flame kindle upon thee.

Isaiah 43:2

Chapter 13 - Day 7

Then they cry unto the LORD in their trouble,
And he saveth them out of their distresses.
He sent his word, and healed them,
And delivered them from their destructions

Psalms 107:19-20

Verily I say unto you,

Whatsoever ye shall bind on earth

Shall be bound in heaven: and

Whatsoever ye shall loose on earth

Shall be loosed in heaven.

Again I say unto you,

That if two of you shall agree on earth

As touching any thing that they shall ask,

It shall be done for them of my

Father which is in heaven.

Matthew 18:18-19

Chapter 13 - Day 7

For verily I say unto you,
That whosoever shall say unto this mountain,
Be thou removed, and be thou cast into the sea;
And shall not doubt in his heart,
But shall believe that those things
Which he saith shall come to pass;
He shall have whatsoever he saith.
Therefore I say unto you,
What things so ever ye desire,
When ye pray, believe that ye receive them,
And ye shall have them.
Mark 11:23-34

And these signs shall follow them that believe;
In my name shall they cast out devils;
They shall speak with new tongues;
They shall take up serpents;
And if they drink any deadly thing,
It shall not hurt them;
They shall lay hands on the sick,
And they shall recover.
Mark 16:17-18

Chapter 13 - Day 7

Prayer

Dear Heavenly Father,
I praise thee oh God! I exalt you above the heavens and the earth! Thou art great oh God, who forgiveth all mine iniquities; who healeth all my diseases. I confess any sin in my heart today. I pray that you will forgive my sins and restore me anew. Thank you for every blessing.

My body is the temple of your Holy Spirit. Please forgive me oh God for allowing any sin, pride, unforgiveness, bitterness, malice, or hatred to open the door for sickness or infirmity.

In the name of Jesus, I break every curse of sickness, disease, infirmity, breast cancer, and premature death from my body and cast it into the sea that it shall come no more.
In the name of Jesus, I bind every foul spirit that wishes to manifest as sickness in my body....every breast cancer cell and cancer producing agents. I loose complete healing, deliverance and restoration over my mind, body, and spirit in Jesus Name. Breast Cancer you must go, in Jesus Name! I speak to miracles, Divine Healing, be released into me in Jesus Name. I know that He that raised up Christ from the dead shall also quicken

Chapter 13 - Day 7

my mortal body by His Spirit that dwells in me.

I believe God's Word for the miracle of Divine Healing in my life. By His stripes, I am healed.

In Jesus Name I pray,
Amen.

Chapter 14

Other TARGETED PRAYERS

Chapter 14

The Lord's Prayer

Our Father which art in heaven,
Hallowed be thy name.
Thy kingdom come,
Thy will be done in earth,
as it is in heaven.
Give us this day our daily bread.
And forgive us our debts,
as we forgive our debtors.
And lead us not into temptation,
but deliver us from evil:
For thine is the kingdom,
and the power,
and the glory,
Forever,
Amen.

Chapter 14

Prayer Before the Biopsy

Be anxious for nothing, but in everything by prayer and supplication, with thanksgiving, let your requests be made known to God; and the peace of God, which surpasses all understanding, will guard your hearts and minds through Christ Jesus.
Phil 4:6-7

"NKJV™"

Chapter 14

Prayer before the Biopsy

Dear Heavenly Father,

I praise thee oh God! I exalt you above the heavens and the earth! Thou art great oh God. Please forgive me for any sin that I may have committed. I am so thankful for every blessing.

God, I am very concerned about the lump in my breast. I pray dear God that you will give me peace and comfort as I prepare for the biopsy.

I pray that you will guide the medical professionals as they withdraw a specimen from my body. Let no germs or sickness enter my body while I am at the medical facility.

Give me strength to live and to walk by faith. I believe that all things work together for the good of those who love you and are called according to your purpose. Hold me dear God while I go through this procedure.

In Jesus Name I pray, Amen

While Waiting for the Biopsy Results

But they that wait upon the LORD shall renew their strength; they shall mount up with wings as eagles; they shall run, and not be weary; and they shall walk, and not faint.

Isaiah 40:31

Chapter 14

While Waiting for the Biopsy Results

Dear Heavenly Father,

I praise thee oh God! I exalt you above the heavens and the earth! Thou art great oh God. Please forgive me for any sin that I may have committed. I am so thankful for every blessing.

God, I am so sorry to be anxious while waiting for the biopsy results. I trust you oh God, but my human mind really wants to know the results. Please give me the patience that I need to wait and be of good courage so that you can strengthen my heart. My faith is strong, and I believe that everything will be according to your will for my life.

I bind every negative thought, every thought of sickness, and every imagination that wishes to enter my mind. I cast it into the pit, and it shall return no more.

I believe that all things work together for the good of those who love you and are called according to your purpose.

Help me to wait with comfort and faith knowing that you have everything in your hands.

In Jesus Name, Amen

Prayer Before Surgery

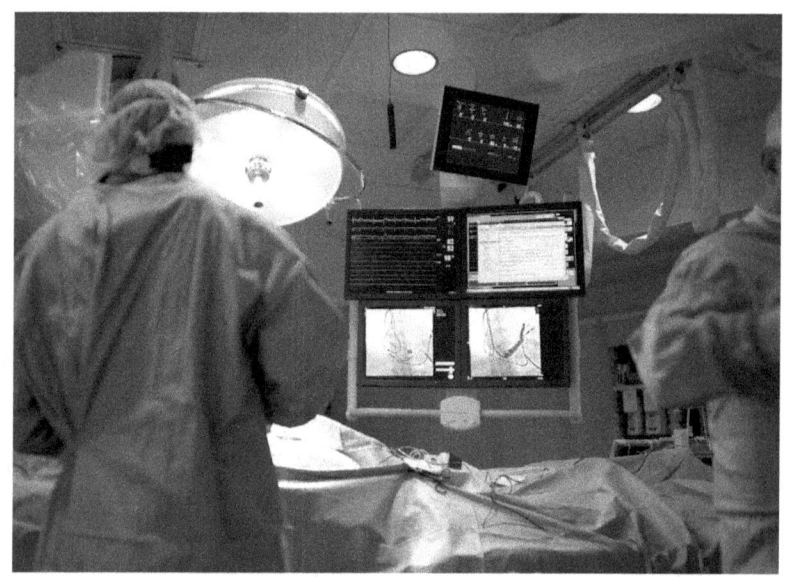

Let us hold fast the profession of our faith
without wavering;
(for he is faithful that promised;)
Hebrews 10:23

Chapter 14

Prayer Before Surgery

Dear Heavenly Father,

I praise thee oh God! I exalt you above the heavens and the earth! Thou art great oh God. Please forgive me for any sin that I may have committed. I am so thankful for every blessing.

God, I know that you created me in your image. I am created in the likeness of God. The biopsy report indicates that cancer cells are present within my body. My faith is strong, for thou can do all but fail. Be with me as I enter surgery. Guide the doctors performing the surgery. Bless them indeed with supernatural abilities to safely remove every infected part in Jesus Name.

Please give comfort to my family, friends, and colleagues while they wait for me during surgery. Let them know that you are with them as you are with me in the operating room. I believe that all things work together for the good of those who love you and are called according to your purpose.

In Jesus Name I pray, Amen

*Beloved, I wish above all things
that thou mayest prosper
and be in health,
even as thy soul prospereth.*

3 John 1:2

www.DivineHealingforBreastCancer.com

www.HealingTestimonial.com

Bibliography

National Institute of Health: Breast Cancer

Unless otherwise noted, all Scripture quotations are from the King James Version of the Bible.

Scripture quotations marked "NKJV™" are taken from the New King James Version®. Copyright © 1982 by Thomas Nelson, Inc. Used by permission. All rights reserved.

Scripture taken from the Amplified Bible, Copyright © 1954, 1958, 1962, 1964, 1965, 1987 by The Lockman Foundation. Used by permission.

Scripture quotations marked (NIV) are taken from the Holy Bible, New International Version®, NIV®. Copyright © 1973, 1978, 1984 by Biblica, Inc.™ Used by permission of Zondervan. All rights reserved worldwide. www.zondervan.com

www.DivineHealingforBreastCancer.com

www.HealingTestimonial.com

About the Author

About the Author

A woman who loves the Lord is a phrase that best describes this author. In addition to her professional duties, Bea is an evangelist, consultant, motivational speaker, workshop leader, conference speaker, wife, mother, and mentor.

Bea was born to a teenage mother. Upon learning of the pregnancy, the teenager's family sent her away. She eventually found a group home for pregnant teenagers. She remained there until the baby was born. Although her family was present for the baby's birth, the little girl (Baby Bea) was immediately placed in the foster care system. After awhile, God blessed Bea with an adoption by the most loving Christian family that you could ever imagine.

She was called into the ministry at an early age. Under the guidance of the Holy Spirit, she delivered her trial sermon at nine years of age. She preached her very first revival at the age of eleven at the Church of God of America in Danville, Kentucky under the tutelage of the late

Bishop A.R. Smith and the late Assistant Bishop Morris A. Napier.

She enlisted as a private. She progressed through the ranks and retired from the United States Army at the rank of Lieutenant Colonel. God chose her to lead people and blessed her with four highly visible command tours of duty. Throughout her years of service to her country, she united in Christian fellowship with believers throughout the nation and around the globe.

Bea firmly believes in the call to prayer. She has witnessed Divine Healings and firmly believes that God will meet you at the point of your need!

> For I know the thoughts that I think toward you, saith the LORD, thoughts of peace, and not of evil, to give you an expected end.
> Jeremiah 29:11

www.DivineHealingforBreastCancer.com

www.HealingTestimonial.com

For Additional Information

For additional information or to schedule Bea for a conference, workshop or speaking engagement:

www.DivineHealingforBreastCancer.com

If you have received Divine Healing for breast cancer, please share your testimony:

www.DivineHealingforBreastCancer.com

If you have experienced Divine Healing in another area, please share your experience:
www.HealingTestimonial.com

I will lift up mine eyes until the hills from whence cometh my help,
All of my help cometh from the Lord.
Psalms 121: 1-2

Dukes Publishing

www.ingramcontent.com/pod-product-compliance
Lightning Source LLC
Chambersburg PA
CBHW070804100426
42742CB00012B/2244